101 Dynamic Sparks

for

Social Media Content

Mostafa Maleki Tehrani

F
×
M

Firouz Media 2024

Firouz Media Limited have contributed to the
publication of this book, while the author retains
full responsibility for copyright, content accuracy,
and any legal matters. This book is a testament to
the author's commitment and enthusiasm, and our
involvement represents a collaborative hybrid effort
in publishing. As you immerse yourself in its
contents, we sincerely hope you find inspiration,
insight, and delight.

ISBN 978-1-915557-20-9
www.firouzmedia.com
IG: @firouzmedia

Cover picture: Bestpixels
Stock images: Pexels_Adobe_Pixabay

101 Dynamic Sparks for Social Media Content
Creator: Mostafa Maleki Tehrani

Preface

In the age of information, people's behaviors have undergone significant changes. In the past, factors such as fixed assets, human resources, or even financial statements were relied upon for validating a business's credibility, and rankings were defined based on these criteria for a company or economic entity.

Today, in the digital era, there are other expressions that can boldly be claimed to be unalterable. Social media platforms are considered among these innovative tools. Nowadays, for customers, the best way to assess a product or service and achieve the desired quality is to look at the number of followers of a provider or read customer comments about good or bad experiences.

Various tools in different areas can either drive customers towards us or drive them away from us, without seeing each other or remembering good and bad experiences. Therefore, our behavior in the virtual space is much more important than observing social norms. A good post on an application can attract a flood of customers towards us, while a bad comment from a customer can act as a barrier to the development of our business.

Moreover, business owners can use these tools to assess their competitors. By seeing a colleague's followers on Instagram, the type of photos shared on Pinterest, or comments on a caption, all these are honest tools for our assessment, as people interact with their real selves in this space. Seth Stephens-Davidowitz, the author of "Everybody Lies," recently said in an interview: "Google is a digital truth serum. People tell Google things they wouldn't tell anyone else, things they might not tell family members, friends, surveyors, or doctors."

Therefore, it is necessary to enter the virtual space with great care and meticulousness. Consequently, this book can provide significant assistance to us.

—Mostafa Maleki Tehrani

WHEN YOU SUPPORT
A SMALL BUSINESS,
YOU'RE SUPPORTING
A DREAM.

"Nature soon takes over if the gardener is absent."

PENELOPE HOBHOUSE

1 Quotation

Happy, inspirational, and motivational quotes always work well.

To Do List

1.

2.

3.

4.

5.

2

Prompting engaging content completion:

With a million dollars, you would _____.

Courtesy of Joseph Mucira

3

Engagement Poll

An effective method to boost interaction.
For instance, "Which of these books is your favorite?"

Courtesy of Cottonbro Studio

4 Behind the Scenes

Sharing a cheerful image of the workspace, photoshoots, or a group picture of the staff.

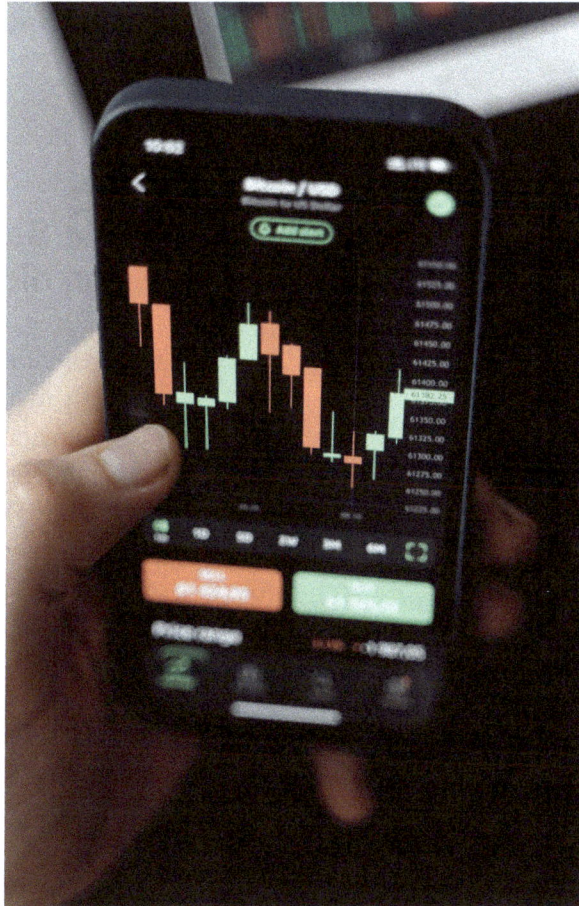

5 Statistics or Data

Sharing recent industry and market statistics with the aim of gathering feedback.

6 Send a link to an old blog post

Potentially driving traffic, improving SEO, sparking engagement, and providing value to your audience. It's a smart way to maximize the use of existing content.

Courtesy of Antoni Shkraba

7 Questions

Pose simple and fundamental questions that your followers can respond to quickly.

What do you consider your top priority or expectation from us?

8 Share a guest post

Distribute thoughtfully curated posts exchanged with one or more other websites.

PRICKLY

PRICKLY STUNNER
NATURAL RED GLOSS IN SECONDS

100% NATURAL PRODUCT   NOT TESTED ON ANIMALS

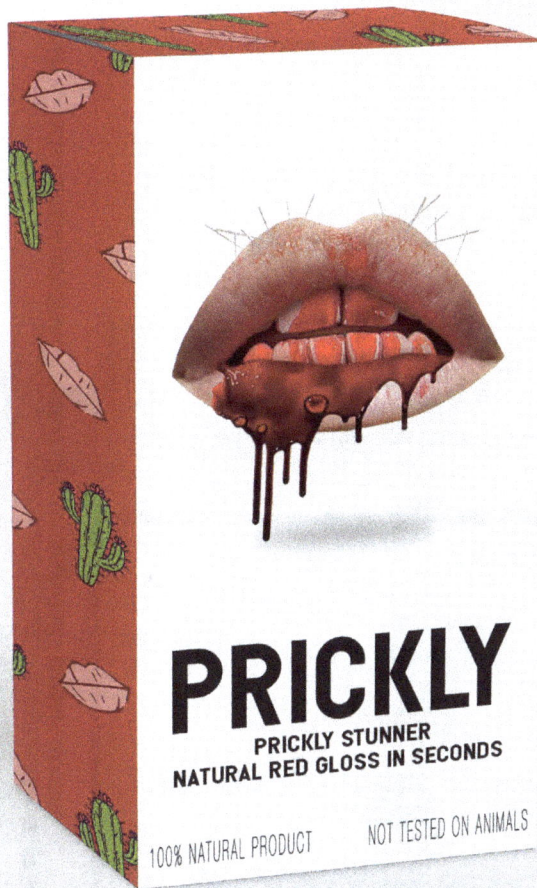

Courtesy of Designecologist

9 Develop and release a brand image

Craft and share a humorous or motivational image featuring your logo or website URL.

10
Infographics

Discover and distribute visually appealing and straightforward infographics centered around topics important to or favored by your followers.

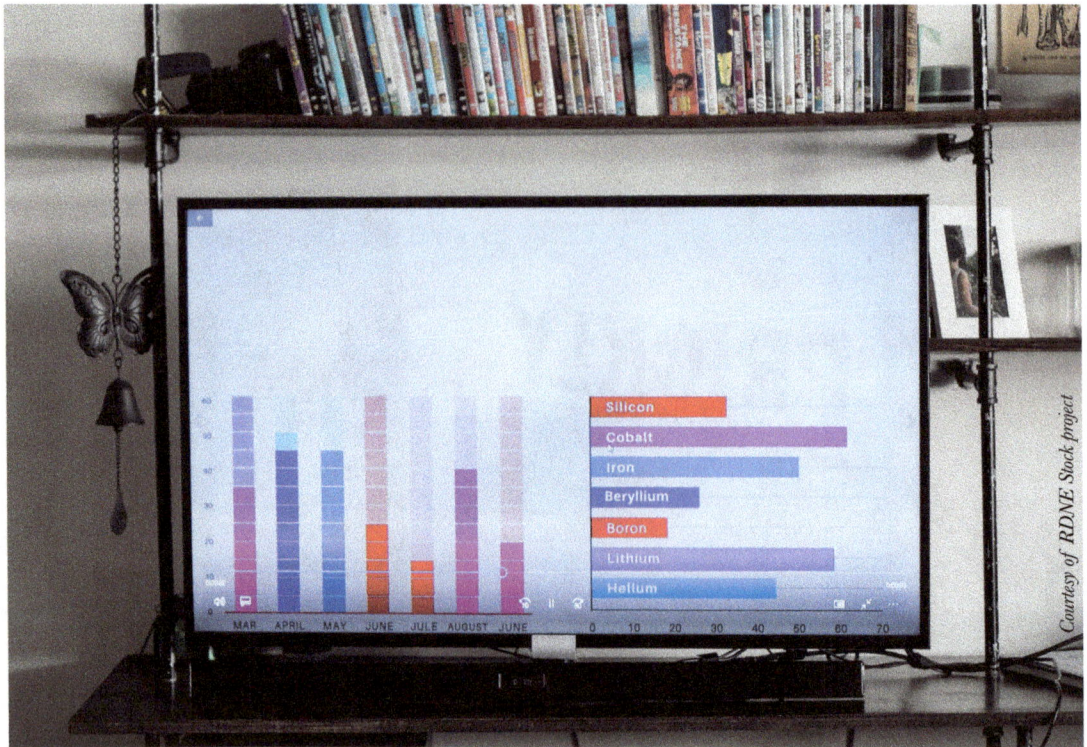

Courtesy of RDNE Stock project

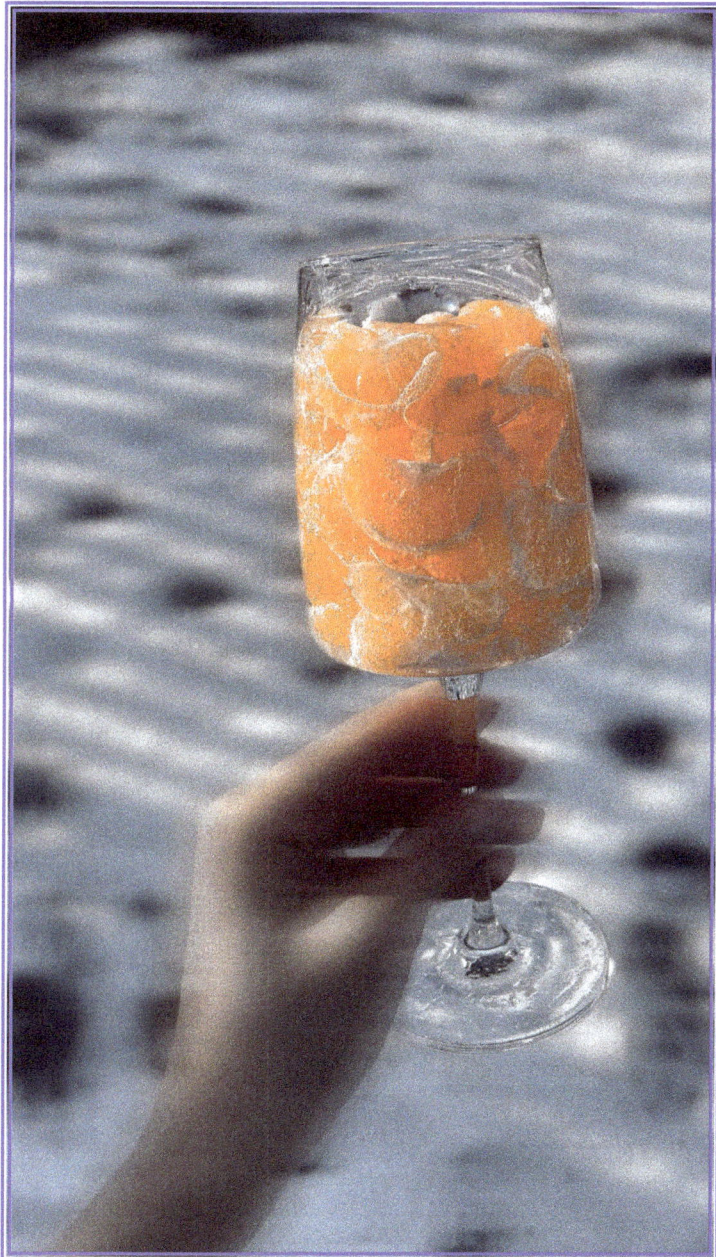

11
Product imagery

Draw inspiration from Pinterest or Instagram to conceptualize and showcase photos of your products and services.

12 Share unrelated product/business photos

Let them convey the emotions embodying your brand.
For instance, the Starbucks Instagram, brand is associated with sunshine, warmth, and camaraderie, not just coffee.

13 Showcase your product's production

Highlight artistic perspectives of individuals, production teams, equipment, and processes.

14 A well-considered challenge surpasses a contentious debate any day.

Instead of engaging in controversial debates, leveraging well-calculated challenges can be more effective for creating thought-provoking content.

From a social media marketing perspective, suppose a fitness brand wants to encourage its followers to adopt a healthier lifestyle. Instead of sparking a debate about various diets or exercise regimens, they could issue a challenge like "30 Days of Fitness" where they invite followers to commit to daily workouts and share their progress. This approach promotes engagement, fosters a sense of community, and encourages positive action among the audience, all while aligning with the brand's messaging and values.

Courtesy of EMilio Mils

Courtesy of Marie

15 Requesting product usage feedback

Encourage your followers to share their thoughts and ideas on
how to enhance your products by using them and providing feedback.

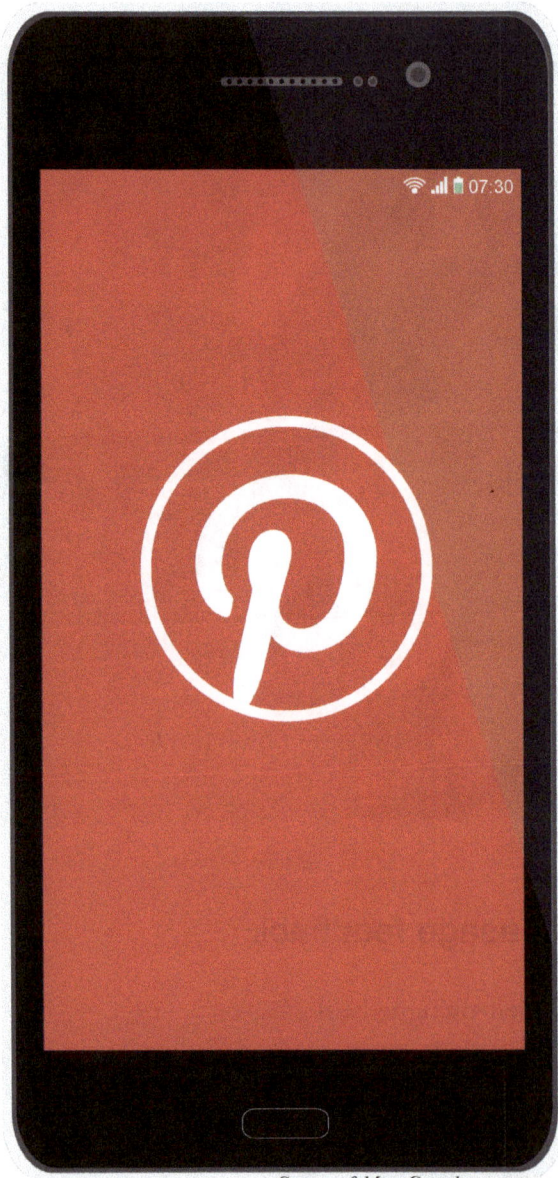

Courtesy of MarcoGonzalez

16
Let Pinterest inspire you

Pinterest is exceptional for finding beautiful images to share as long as we adhere to intellectual property laws.

17 Share valuable resources

This fosters engagement through an exchange of information, encouraging reciprocal interactions..

Manfred Steger

18

Distribute a Slideshare presentation

Utilize Slideshare as a platform to disseminate concise yet impactful presentations that effectively communicate key messages and valuable information to your target audience.

19 Link to a case study

Present case studies detailing the product or service provided.

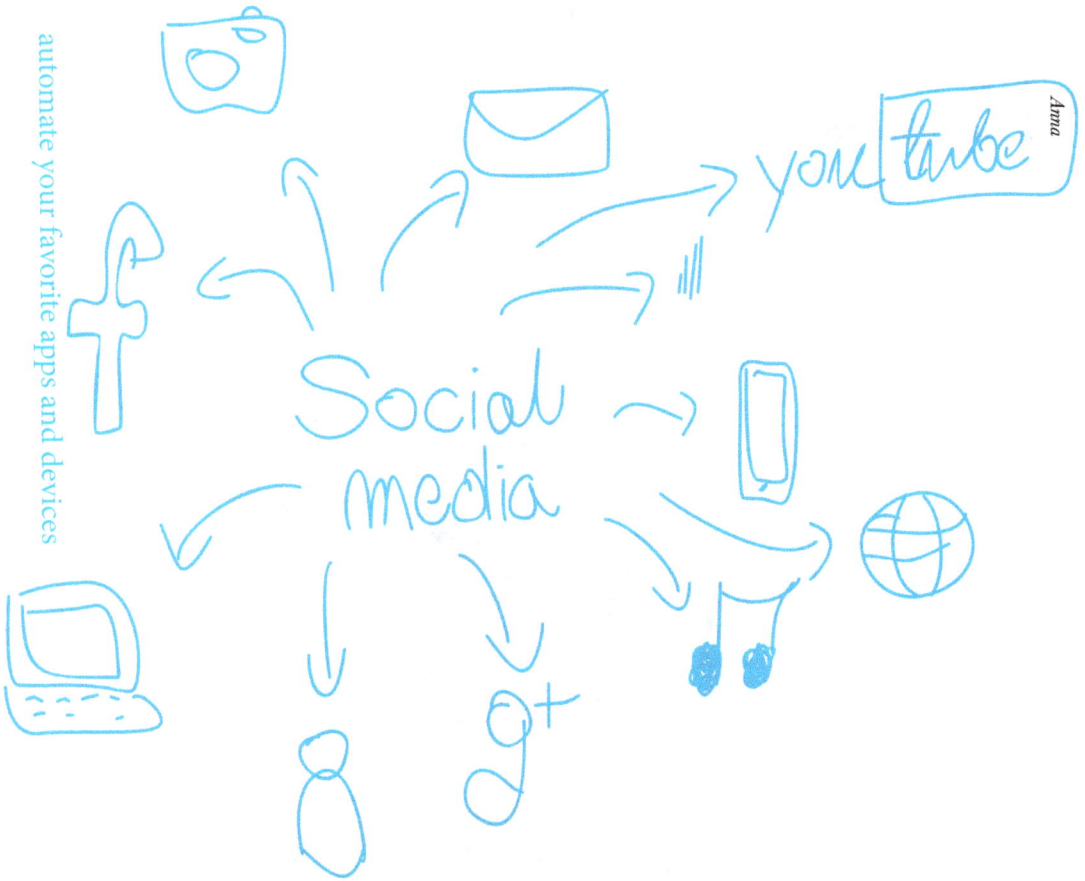

20 Link to a relevant IFTTT applet

Connect with an IFTTT applet pertinent to your industry, facilitating seamless integration across all social media platforms.

21
Ask for reviews or descriptions

Seeking followers' opinions is among the most effective ways to gather descriptions that can serve as social proof on your website.

geralt

Courtesy of Cottombro Studio

22

Fan photos

Explore pertinent hashtags associated with your business or products, then showcase a customer's photo on Facebook or Pinterest.

- User-generated content
- Engagement
- Community building
- Visual appeal
- Reach and exposure

23

Recommend a tool

Suggest useful tools or
resources, preferably free,
that you believe would benefit
your followers.

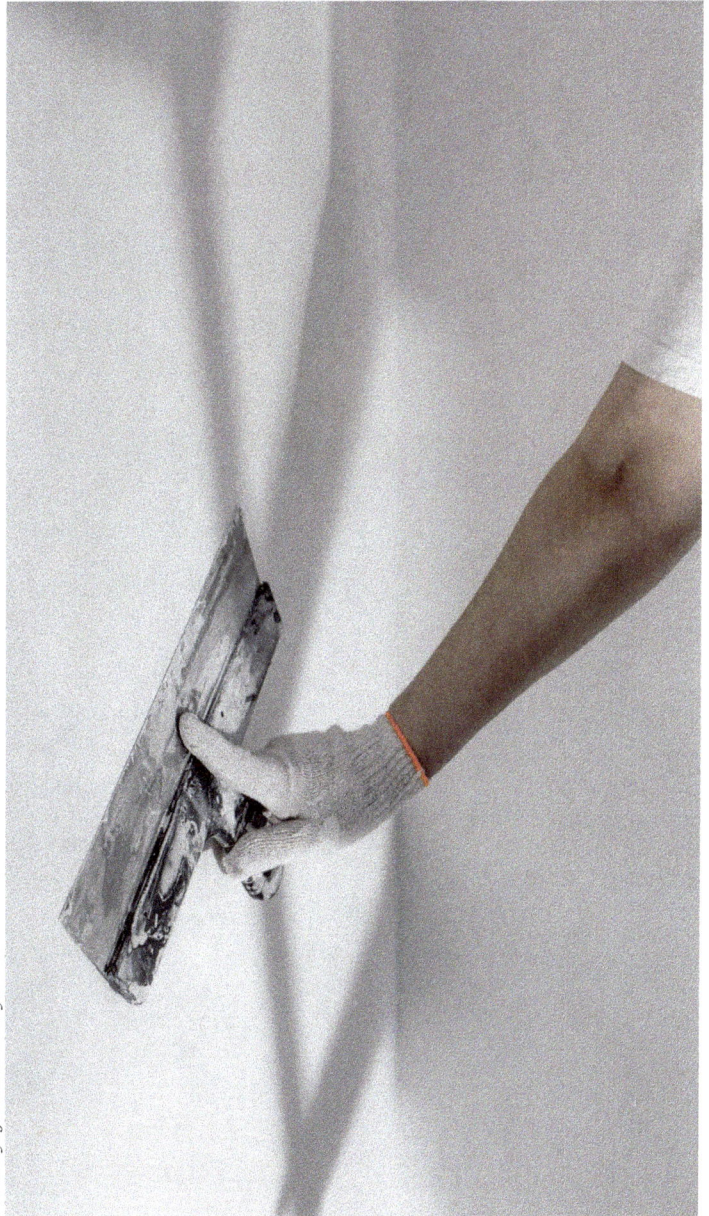

Courtesy of Ksenia Chernaya

24 Share a favorite book

Posts a book to provide value, demonstrate expertise, encourage engagement, and diversify content.

Courtesy of Cotombro Studio

Courtesy of Lisa Fotios

25
Daily Publishing

Share a post about your daily life, highlighting topics that
resonate with your followers' interests.

26 Recommend your preferred products

For e-commerce sites, showcase a compilation of best-selling items or products with top ratings.

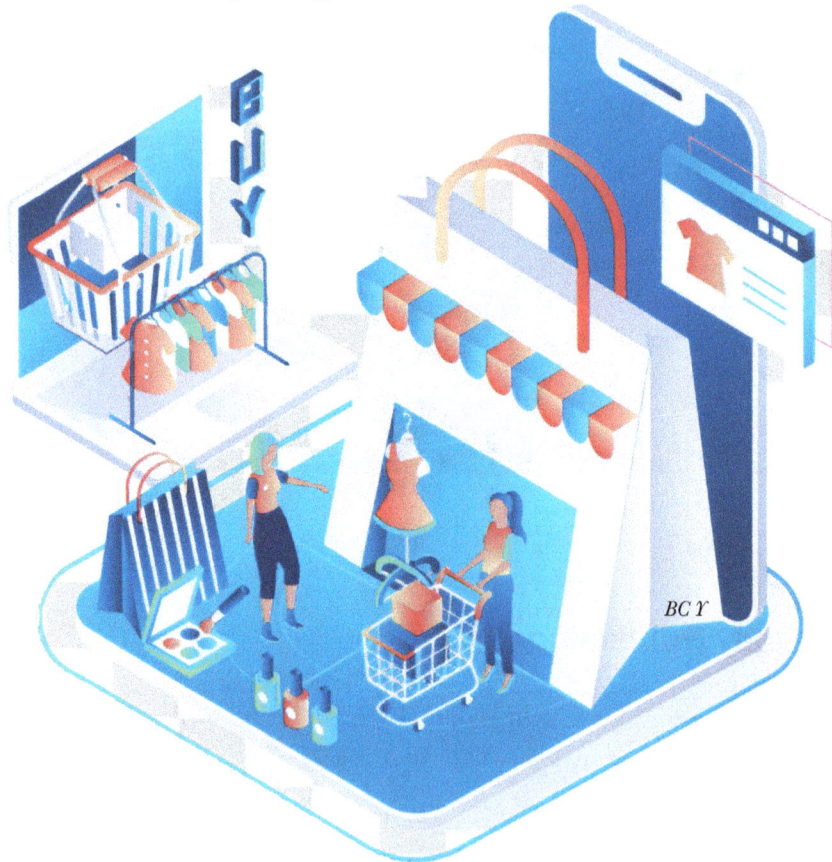

27 Share random tips

Regularly dispatch a newsletter or tip that offers practical value to your followers. Incorporating random numbers, such as "Example Tip #256," adds significance to your post.

Courtesy of Sabine Kroschel

28 Link to your top-performing blog post

Provide a brief introduction detailing why your post has garnered significant readership and shares.

Pixabay

29 Entrepreneurial Guidance

Share your successful past entrepreneurial experiences to inspire and ignite passion.

30 Offer a work-life balance tip

Demonstrate authenticity to your social media followers by sharing a personal lesson learned in juggling work, life, and family responsibilities.

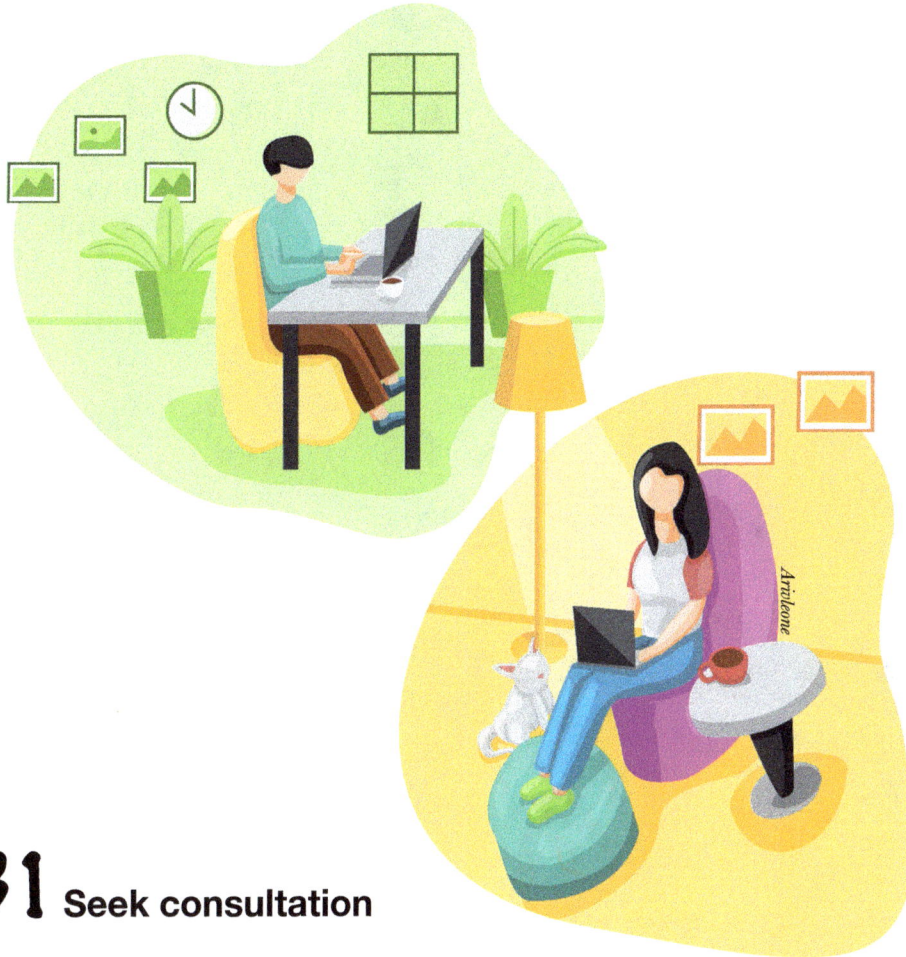

31 Seek consultation

Present a hypothetical scenario and inquire about the course of action your followers would pursue in such circumstances.

32

Journey through business history

Rediscover the past by sharing nostalgic photos of old brands, websites, or your initial product. Take your followers a quick trip down memory lane!

33

Authentic posts showcasing your human side

Share snippets of your daily life, like last night's dinner or weekend plans, to demonstrate authenticity and relatability.

34 Reddit

Share the top-performing Reddit link relevant to your industry or an intriguing event, such as renowned personalities engaging in an 'Ask Me Anything' session.

WeDevlops_com

Shari Jo

Gerd Altmann

35 Follow social media recommendations

Share a link to another user's social media profile and encourage your followers to give them a follow.

36

Share a Pinterest post from your followers

If your customers are active on Pinterest, consider sharing one of their posts.

BFC SOFTTECH

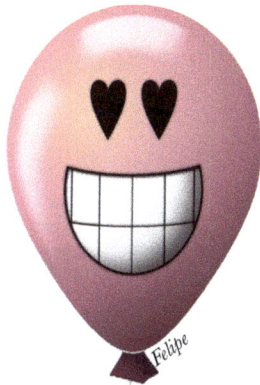

37

Share a comic or melody

Fostering laughter with your audience is an excellent method for cultivating connections.

Felipe

Courtesy of Rheo/Pixabay

38 Share a video

Share a video, or even better, invite your social media followers to submit their own videos.

Encouraging user-generated videos is crucial for social media marketing:

- Engagement: Boosts interaction and connection.
- Authenticity: Adds genuine perspectives.
- Community: Strengthens bonds among followers.
- Variety: Diversifies content for interest.
- Social Proof: Demonstrates product value effectively.

Courtesy of Julia M Cameron

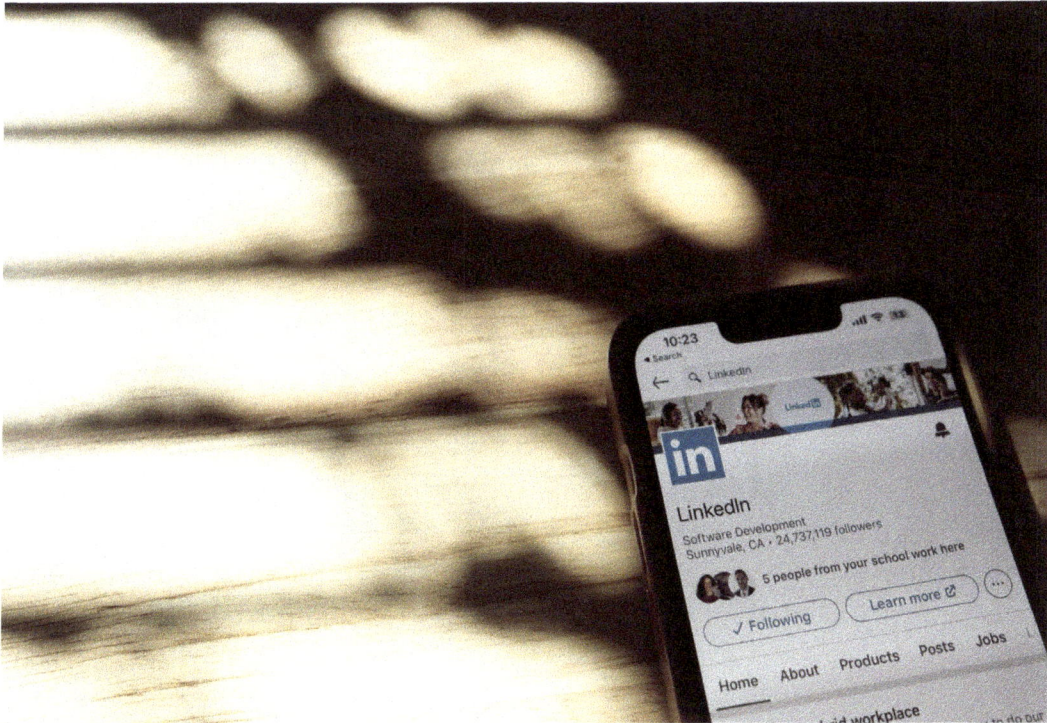

Courtesy of Airam Dato-on

39 LinkedIn colleague recommendation

Enhance your communication skills to connect with valuable resources.

Sharpen your communication skills to form genuine connections with knowledgeable individuals. Effective communication builds trust, encourages collaboration, and maximizes your professional network's potential.

40

Hosting a photo contest

Encourage fans to submit passion-driven photos and prompt followers to vote for their favorites. Spread positivity by celebrating the selection of winning photos.

Courtesy of Lisa Fotios

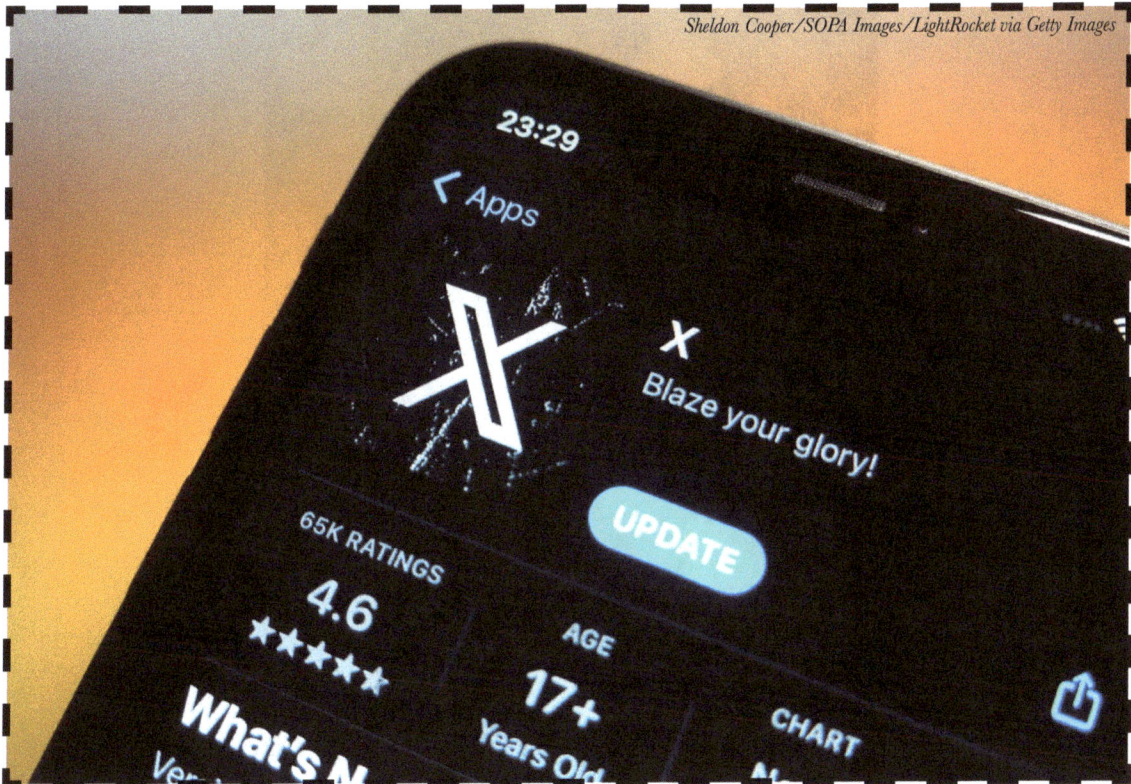

41 Share a X trend

Utilize analytics tools to discover trending topics related to X, and distribute them.

Monitor keywords, URLs, social media handles, and more, tracking mentions and keywords across various platforms including news, blogs, and forums.

Courtesy of Canva Studio

42

Discussion Forum

Establish a forum for engaging with followers, facilitating discussions, and exchanging opinions.

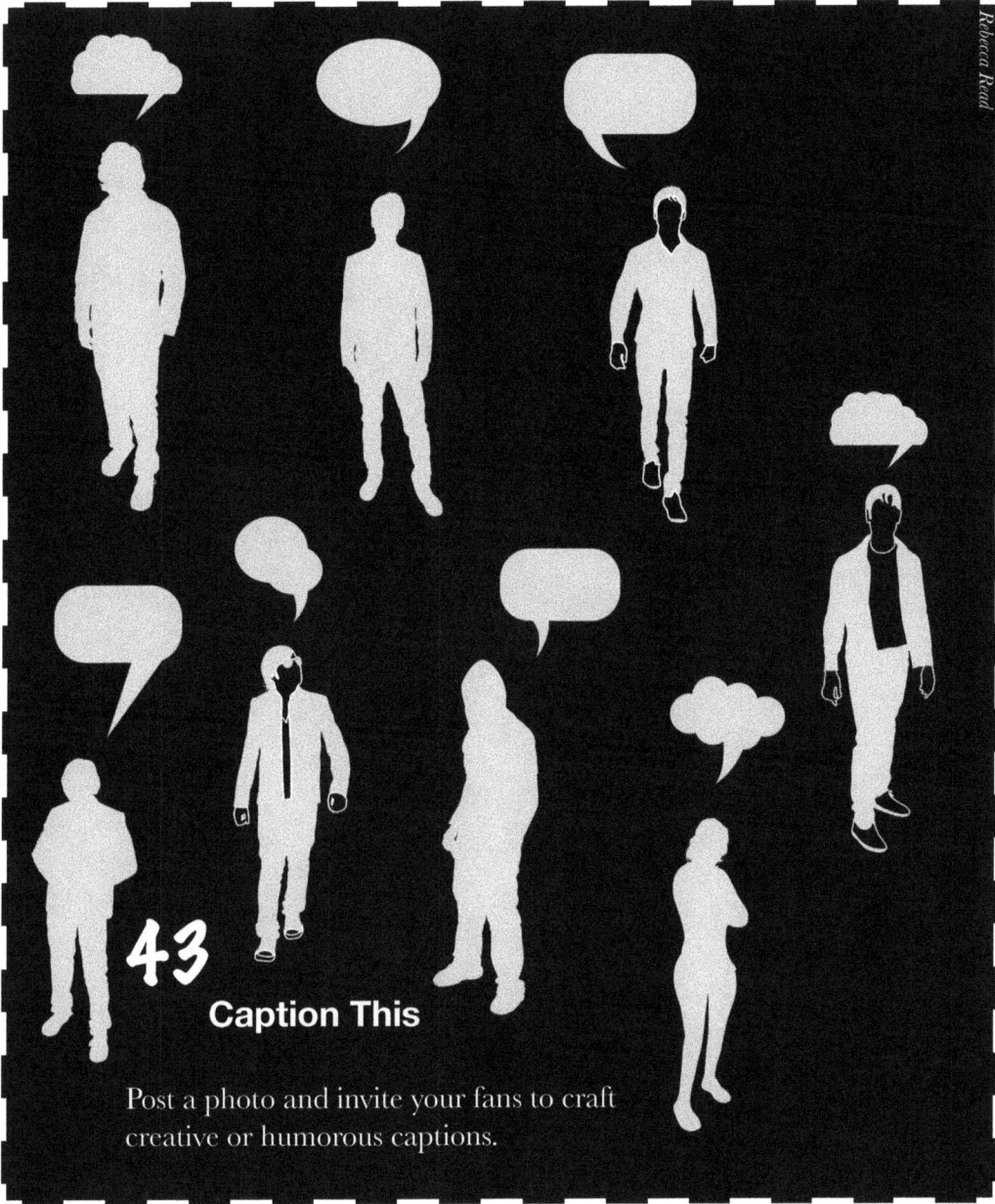

43

Caption This

Post a photo and invite your fans to craft creative or humorous captions.

44 YouTube Video

Discover a captivating or motivational video, and share it with your fans or followers.

Courtesy of Gerd Altmann

45 Tag another Facebook page

Promote another business by showcasing their good deeds and create more opportunities for collaboration.

Tagging another Facebook page is important because it:

- Increases visibility.
- Builds relationships.
- Facilitates cross-promotion.
- Boosts community engagement.

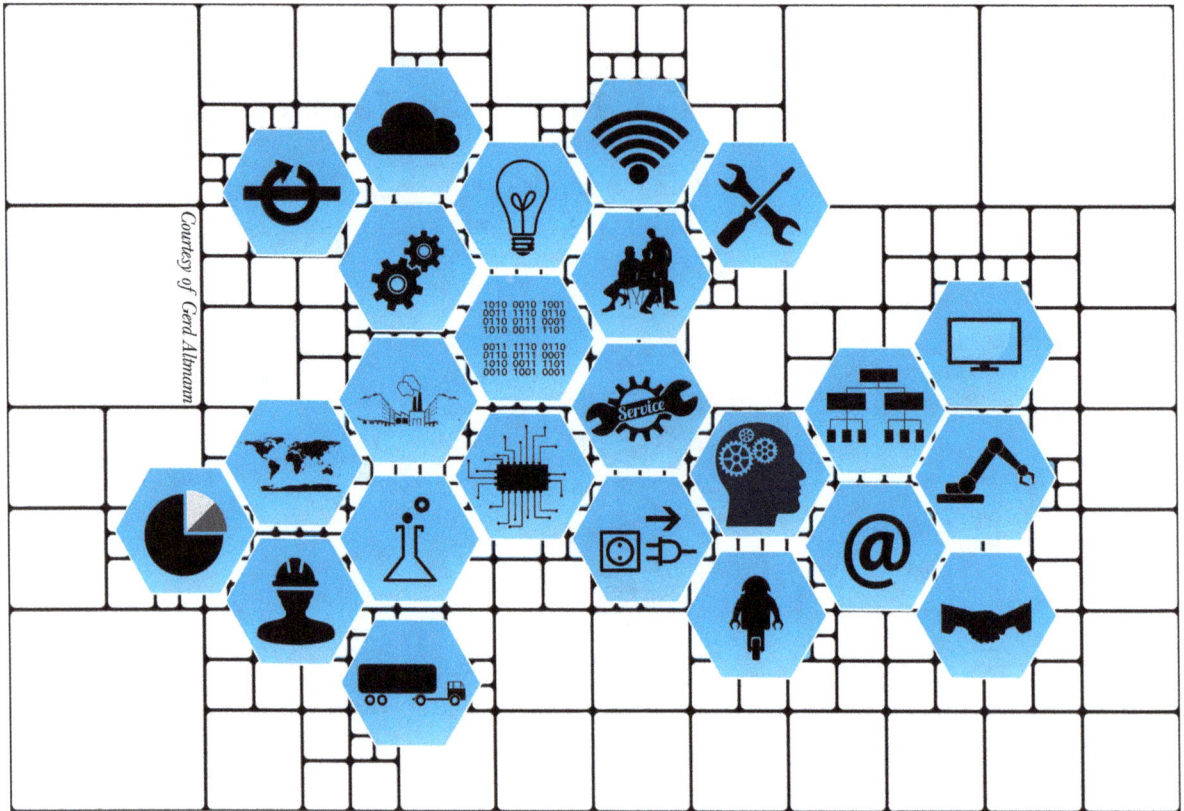

Courtesy of Gerd Altmann

46
Industry-related news

Distributing updates about the sector or services within the industry.

- Keeps you relevant.
- Engages your audience.
- Builds authority.
- Diversifies content.
- Educates customers.

Gerd Altmann

- Broadens reach.
- Shows cultural sensitivity.
- Enhances brand image.
- Boosts engagement.
- Strengthens relationships.

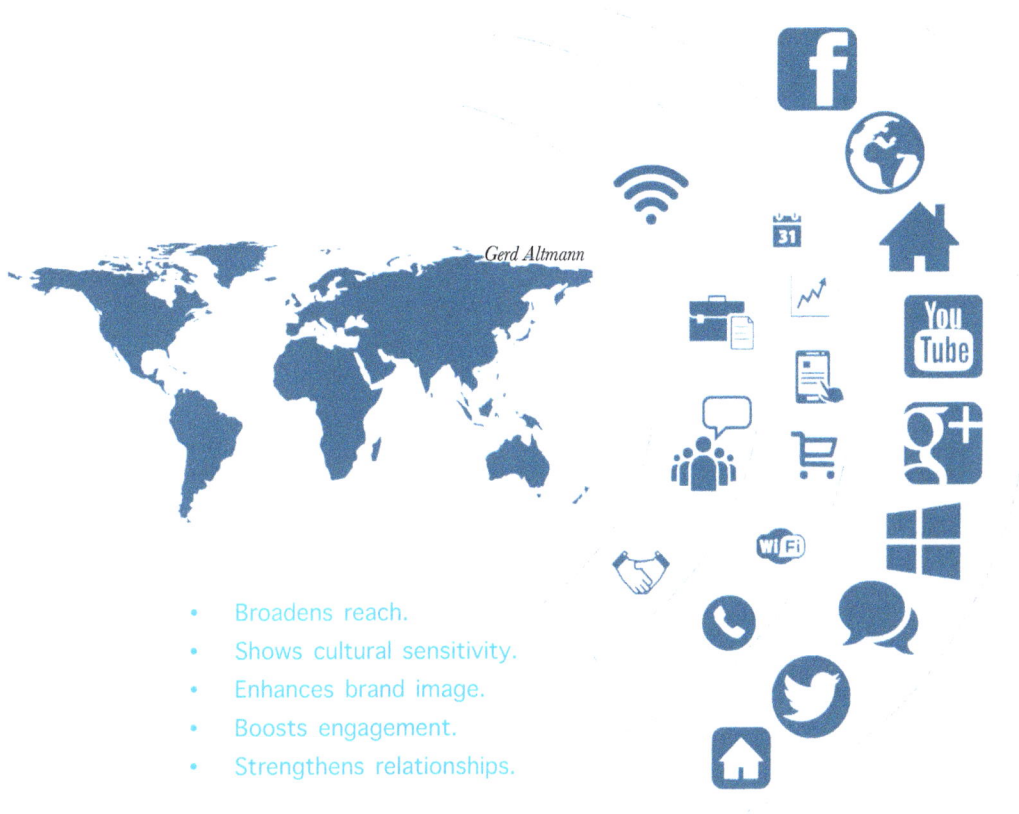

47 Celebrate global customs and special occasions

Delight followers worldwide by acknowledging their national days or special occasions, fostering a sense of inclusivity and connection.

48

Anticipating an Upcoming Event

Engage your followers by asking for their predictions. Let's hear what everyone thinks. Share your insights.

For example: Get ready to cheer! My forecast is that Germany will clinch the World Cup victory. How about you? Share your predictions! #WorldCup #GermanyForTheWin

Pixabay

49
Offering a free e-book

Sending a complimentary e-book to your customers' email addresses.

Offering a free e-book and sending it to customers' emails is crucial for marketing because it generates leads, builds trust, fosters engagement, allows for upselling, collects valuable data, encourages word-of-mouth, and provides long-term brand value.

Courtesy of Cottonbro Studio

50
Ask questions

Let your fans ask anything they want.

Encouraging fan questions is crucial in marketing:

Engagement: Questions prompt active participation, fostering engagement.
Insights: Fans' inquiries offer valuable insights for strategy and content.
Community: It builds a sense of community, fostering dialogue.
Transparency: Demonstrates openness, enhancing brand trust.
Content Ideas: Questions inspire future content across platforms.
Customer Service: Provides a platform for responsive support.
Buzz Generation: Public engagement amplifies brand visibility.

Overall, it's a potent tactic for engagement, insights, community, transparency, content, service, and buzz.

Pixabay

51 Share provocative statement

Be the actor defending the devil, but listen carefully.
This prompts curiosity, encourages active listening, sparks dialogue, evokes emotions, sets your brand apart, and creates shareable content.

52 Utilize Facebook interest lists for content inspiration.

Use Facebook interest lists to understand your audience's preferences. Share relevant content or create your own based on their interests. Encourage interaction and refine your strategy over time.

53 Employee profile

Let your followers know that they're interacting with real people, not a bot.

Connection
Authenticity
Trust Building
Expertise Display
Employee Advocacy
Encourages Engagement

Hello, listeners!
Welcome to the today's show...

Courtesy of Joseph Mucira

54
Communication for product reminders

Stay attentive for product feedback to stay ahead of the curve.

Courtesy of Joseph Mucira

Courtesy of Joseph Mucira

55
Fact or Fiction

Try this engaging post for your followers: "Can eating carrots really improve night vision? Share your guess in our 'Fact or Fiction' challenge!"

56

Share a trending topic from Google searches.

Explore Google's trending searches to discover popular topics. Choose one to focus on and tailor your content accordingly

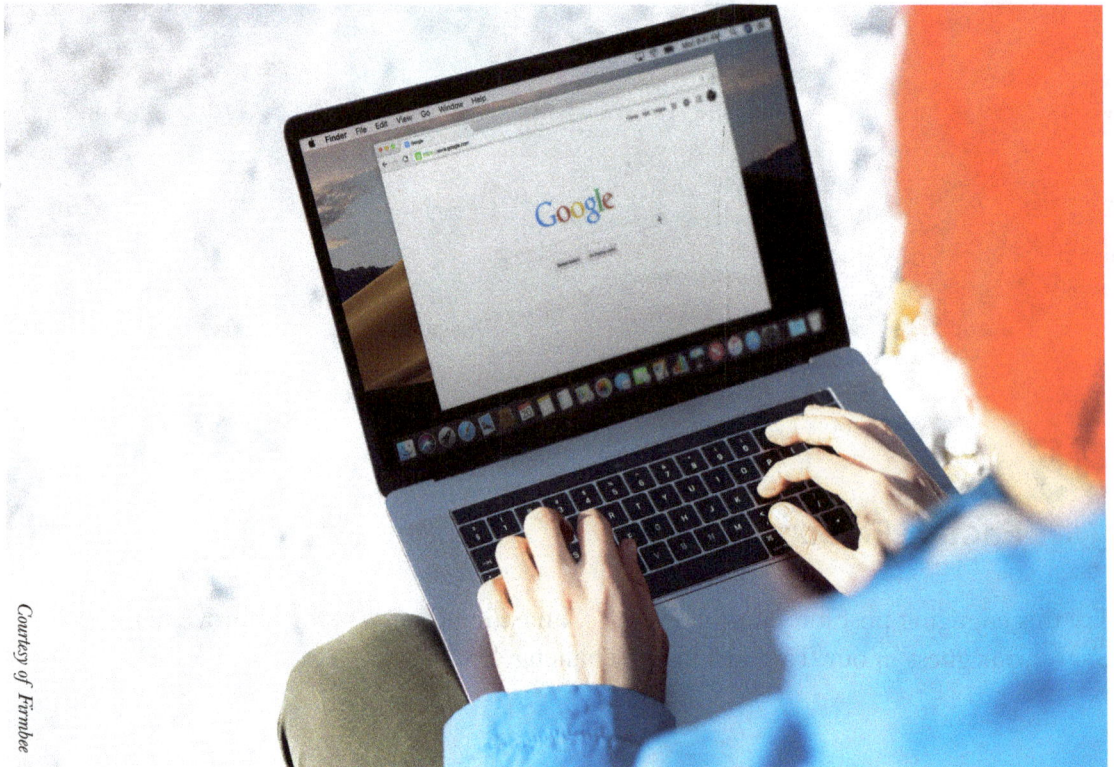

57
Introducing your top ambassador of the month

Highlighting your top ambassador of the month validates their efforts and shows appreciation for their support of your brand.

58 Sharing industry and service research

Sharing research findings and summaries with your followers can provide valuable insights.

59 Drive quick sales

Boost rapid sales by leveraging platforms such as Snapchat to provide exclusive, limited-time coupons. Create urgency, target a responsive audience, engage customers directly, and provide measurable results for optimization.

Joseph Mucira

Courtesy of Nataliya Vaikevich

60

Quirky and unusual celebrations

Discover quirky celebrations like "Apple Strudel Day" on June 17th using tools like Days of the Year to celebrate unique festivities.

61 | Awards or certificates you've received

Share your awards or certificates with care, focusing on building trust rather than simply showcasing achievements. This demonstrates your expertise, credibility, and achievements, inspiring others and establishing you as a leader in your field. Therefore, sharing these accolades isn't just about boasting; it's about reinforcing your reputation and credibility.

Courtesy of Michael Steinberg

Courtesy of Ola Dapo

62

Promote others' sales

Promote others' sales by sharing a coupon or sale link from a non-competing business. This drives traffic their way and fosters goodwill, potentially leading to future support.

63

Latest company updates

Any changes happening in your business? New team members joining? Revised operating hours? Exciting new product launches?

Sharing company updates keeps everyone informed about changes, engages your audience, maintains relevance, enhances customer service, and promotes new offerings.

Courtesy of Cottonbro Studio

64
Sharing images from a recent industry event

When sharing images from a recent industry event, remember to boost visibility by using the relevant event hashtag for greater exposure.

Courtesy of Eduardo Romero

65
Free download

Offer a complimentary download, whether it's a plugin, wallpaper, e-book, or anything else beneficial to your audience.

Courtesy of Kaboompics

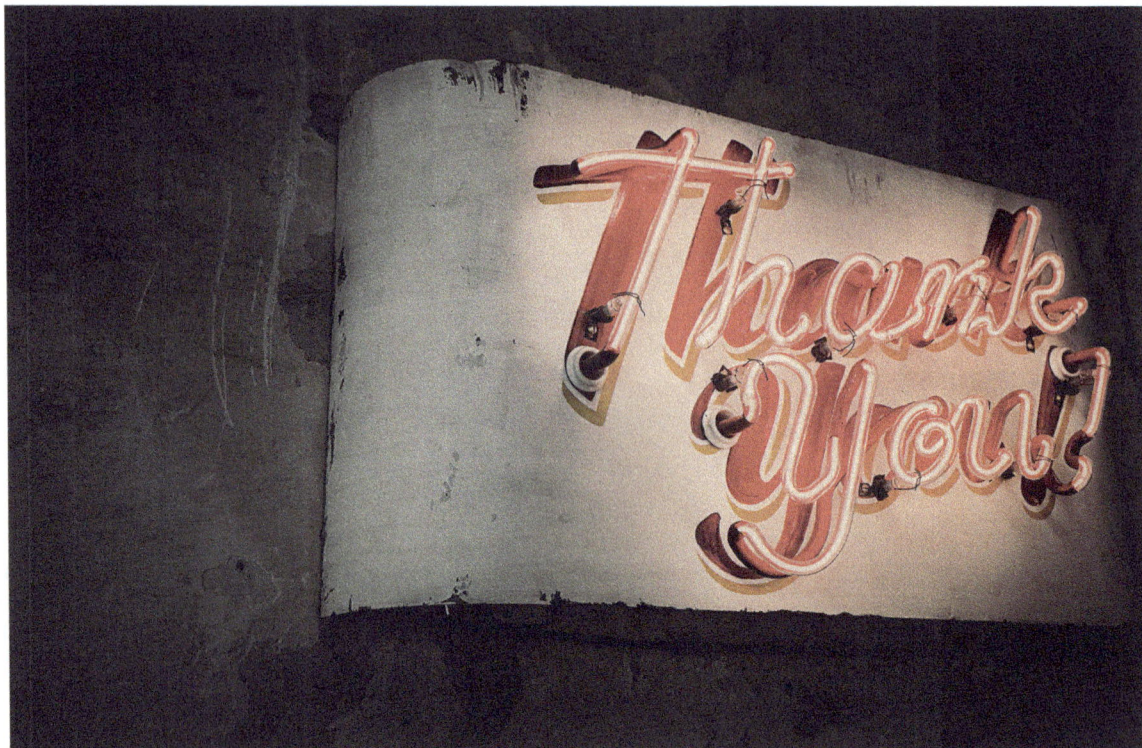

Courtesy of Ryan McGuire

66
Thanking your fans

Expressing gratitude to your fans goes a long way in building
connections with your followers.

67
Offering an expert opinion

Providing an expert opinion can be greatly
impactful, showcasing your leadership skills
and competence visually.

Courtesy of Tumisu

Courtesy of Gerd Altmann

68 Craft social media posts akin to your blog content.

From a social media standpoint:

Consistency: Share blog-like posts for brand coherence.
Reach: Expand audience via social media.
Engagement: Foster real-time interaction.
Visuals: Use captivating content.
Call to Action: Drive action with clear prompts.
Analytics: Refine strategy based on insights.
Storytelling: Humanize brand with behind-the-scenes content.

In summary, blend blog-like posts into social media for coherence, reach, engagement, visuals, action, analytics, and storytelling.

69

Weekly article compilation post

Distribute a curated list of articles for the week.

Courtesy of Liza Summer

70

Ask your employees to post

Your employees can present a more
accurate picture of what goes on to
the audience.

71

Stories

Try incorporating storytelling into your posts to create emotional connections with your audience and make your brand more relatable.

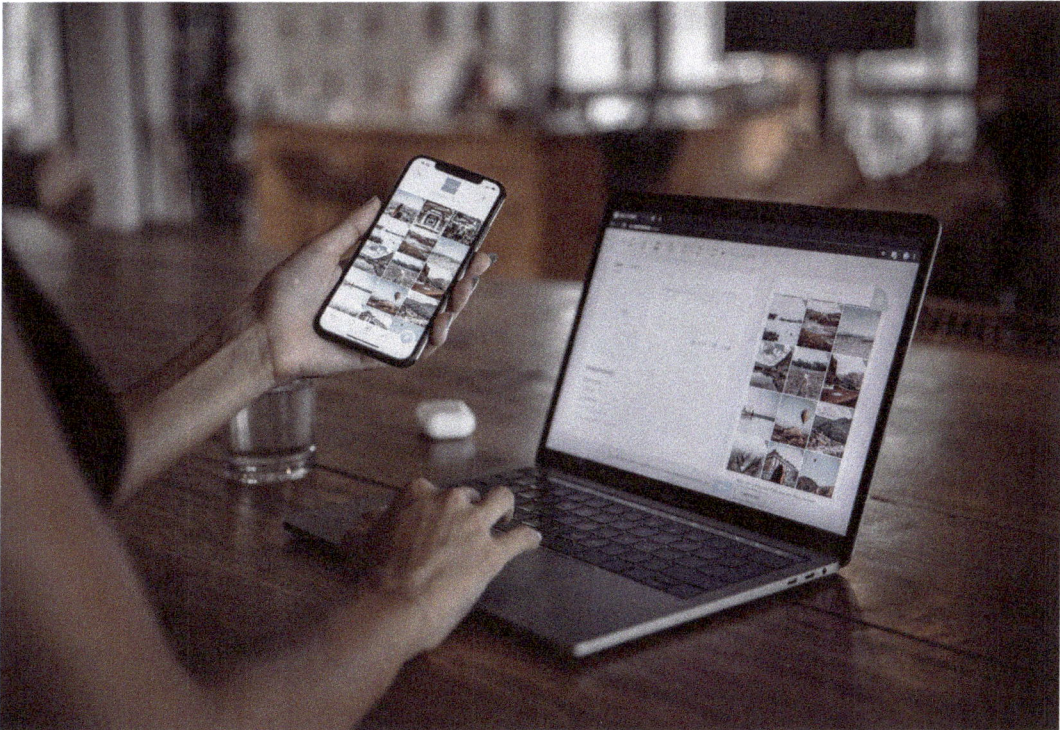

Courtesy of Plann

Courtesy of Polina Zimmerman

72
Host a webinar

Host a webinar and advertise it across your social media platforms. Google Hangouts is recommended for hosting.

Promoting your webinar on social media matters because it expands your reach, boosts engagement, increases visibility, raises brand awareness, facilitates networking, and gathers valuable feedback.

73
Campaign

Promote an event and encourage followers to participate, such as participating in a charity fundraiser or volunteering for a community clean-up initiative.

By participating in such events, followers contribute to meaningful causes, build connections with like-minded individuals, and align themselves with brands that prioritize social responsibility. This not only benefits the community and the causes being supported but also creates a sense of purpose and fulfillment for you and your followers.

Courtesy of Fauxels

74
Quote from your industry expert

Seek insights from an industry expert by posing a question, then share their response on social media.

Courtesy of Ivan Kot

$\boldsymbol{75}$ Make a request

Requesting action from your audience is crucial for engagement. Be clear about what you're asking them to do and why it matters. Provide context for your request, express gratitude for their participation, and inspire them to take action.

Courtesy of Gerd Altmann

76 Display a unique finesse.

Demonstrate finesse by subtly introducing a gesture, such as a blog post, contest launch, or product unveiling, to delight your enthusiasts and fans.

Courtesy of Ron Lach

Courtesy of Los Muertos Crew

77 Interview

Conduct a dialogue with an industry expert to glean insights and expertise.

78

A photo collage

Sharing a photo collage created with tools like PicMonkey adds visual interest to your content and enhances its appeal. It allows you to showcase multiple images in a creative and organized manner, effectively conveying your message or story. Additionally, using such tools simplifies the process of creating and editing collages, ensuring that your content looks polished and professional.

Courtesy of Picjumbo

79
Teasing content

Provide teaser content without revealing the punchline to pique curiosity and boost views. Teaser content matters because it generates curiosity and anticipation, prompting viewers to engage further with your content in order to discover more. This can lead to increased views, engagement, and ultimately, interest in your brand or message.

Courtesy of Brett Sayles

80 Industry events

Anticipate upcoming industry events and predict trends within your niche market. Forecasting industry events matters because it allows you to stay ahead of the curve and prepare for upcoming changes or developments in your niche. By predicting trends, you can position your business to capitalize on opportunities and mitigate potential risks. Additionally, forecasting helps you to stay competitive by understanding market dynamics and adapting your strategies accordingly. This proactive approach enables you to make informed decisions and stay relevant in a rapidly evolving industry landscape.

Courtesy of Matheus Bertelli

81 Share a novel and unexpected way to use your productw

Share an innovative and surprising new application for your product, and encourage your followers to share their own ideas as well.

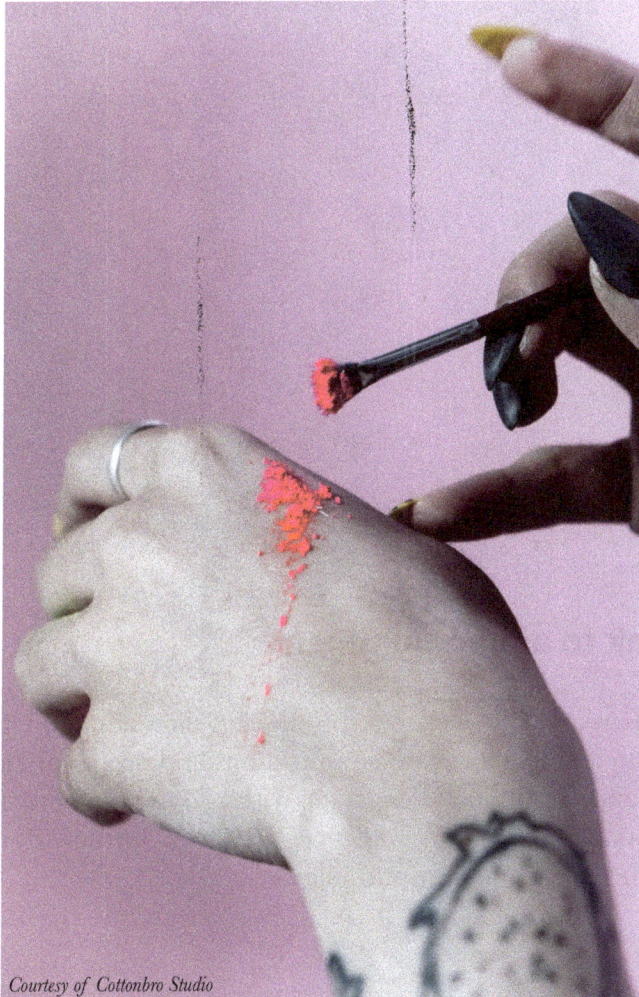

Courtesy of Cottonbro Studio

Courtesy of Ivan Samkov

82 Link to a blog comment

Direct your fans and followers to a specific blog comment and invite them to engage with it. This can spark conversations and deepen their connection with your brand. Additionally, engaging with comments demonstrates that you value and appreciate your audience's feedback, further strengthening the relationship between you and your followers.

83 Respond to commonly asked questions.

Address common inquiries by sharing answers on social media.

Demonstrates your commitment to customer service and helps to alleviate concerns or confusion among your audience. By addressing these inquiries on social media, you provide quick and accessible solutions, improving the overall customer experience.

Courtesy of Ivan Samkov

84 Provide access to past newsletters by sharing a link

Share archived newsletters with new subscribers, ensuring they have access to past content.

Courtesy of StockSnap

85 Ask fans for content ideas and discover their needs

Engage your fans by asking for content ideas and identifying the issues or problems they need help with. Engaging fans for content ideas and understanding their needs is crucial for tailoring your content strategy to their interests and addressing their concerns effectively.

86 Share a link to a useful Facebook or LinkedIn group

Sharing a helpful Facebook or LinkedIn group with your followers is beneficial because it provides them with access to valuable resources and networking opportunities within their professional or interest-based communities.

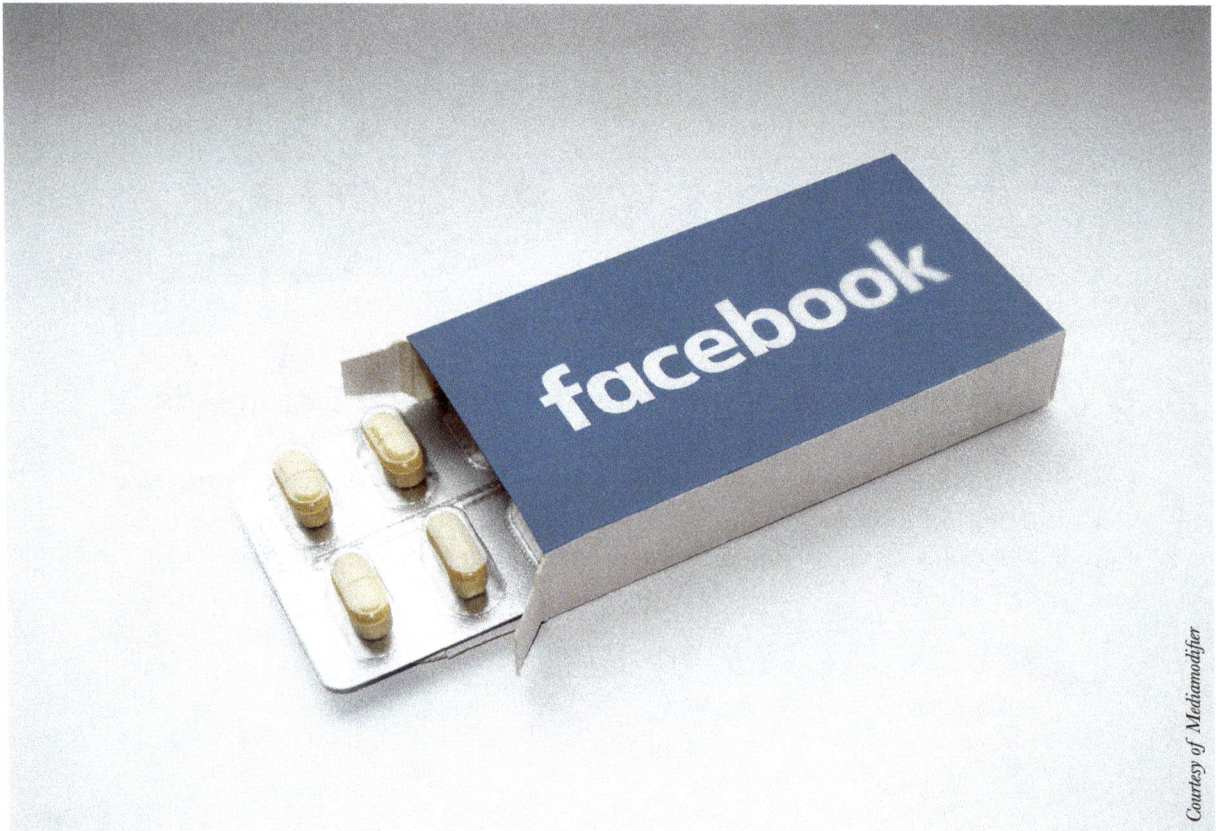

Courtesy of Mediamodifier

87
Tell a story

Share a funny or interesting story from your own life.

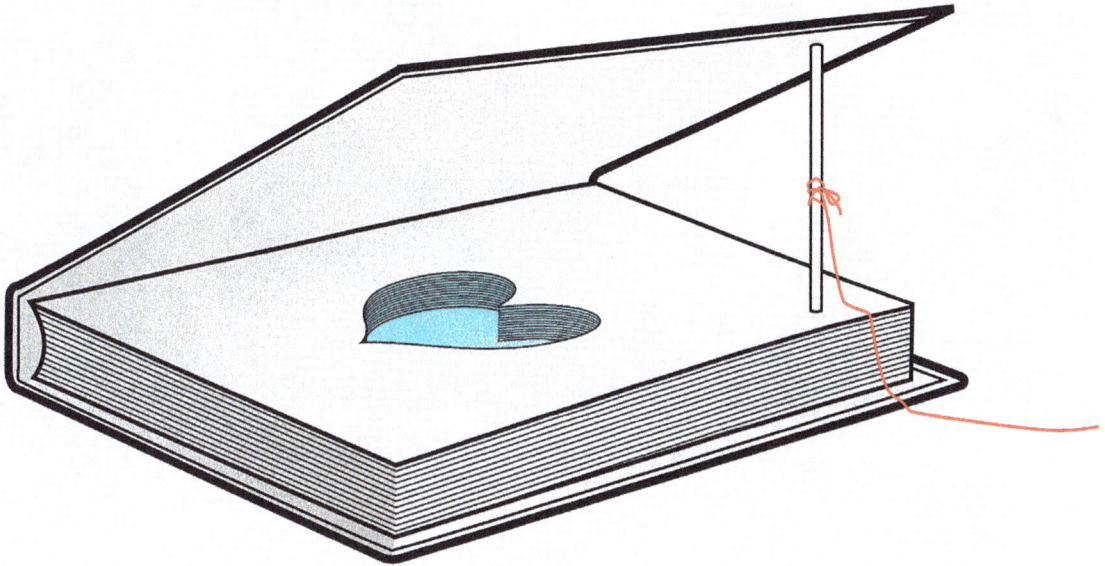

Sharing personal stories matters because it humanizes your brand, allowing your audience to connect with you on a deeper level. It fosters authenticity, relatability, and emotional resonance, strengthening the bond between you and your audience. Additionally, storytelling is a powerful way to captivate attention, convey messages, and make content more memorable and engaging. By sharing stories, you can create meaningful connections, inspire empathy, and ultimately, build trust and loyalty with your audience.

Courtesy of Moondance

88

Enhance your social media strategy by learning from your competitors.

Improve by analyzing and outperforming your competitors' social media strategies, easily done with tools like Social Crawlytics.

89 Use website analytics for content inspiration

Use website analytics to uncover content ideas. Identify topics of interest to create resonant content for your audience.

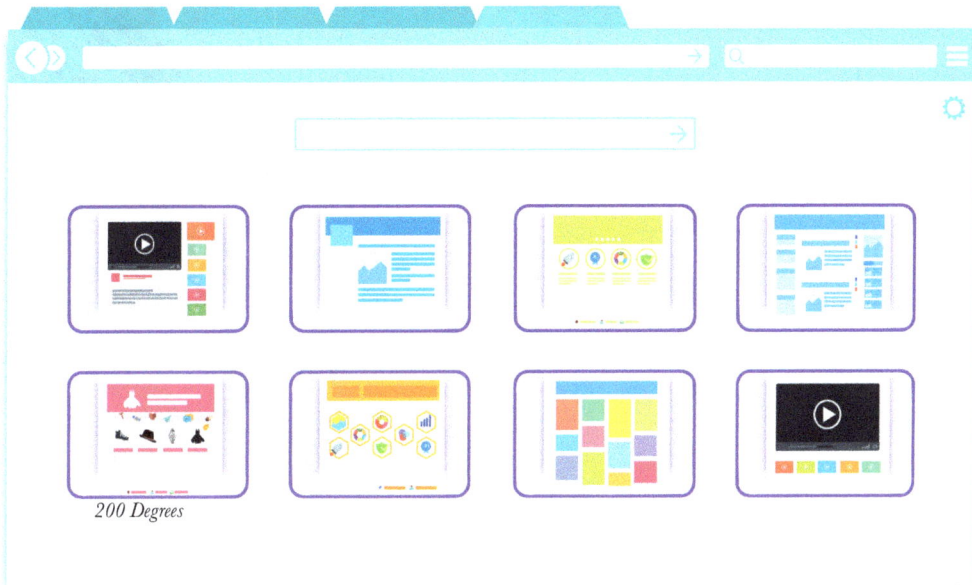

200 Degrees

90
Q&A

Holding a live Q&A session.

This allows for direct interaction with your audience, fostering engagement and building relationships. It provides an opportunity to address questions, concerns, and interests in real-time, demonstrating responsiveness and transparency.

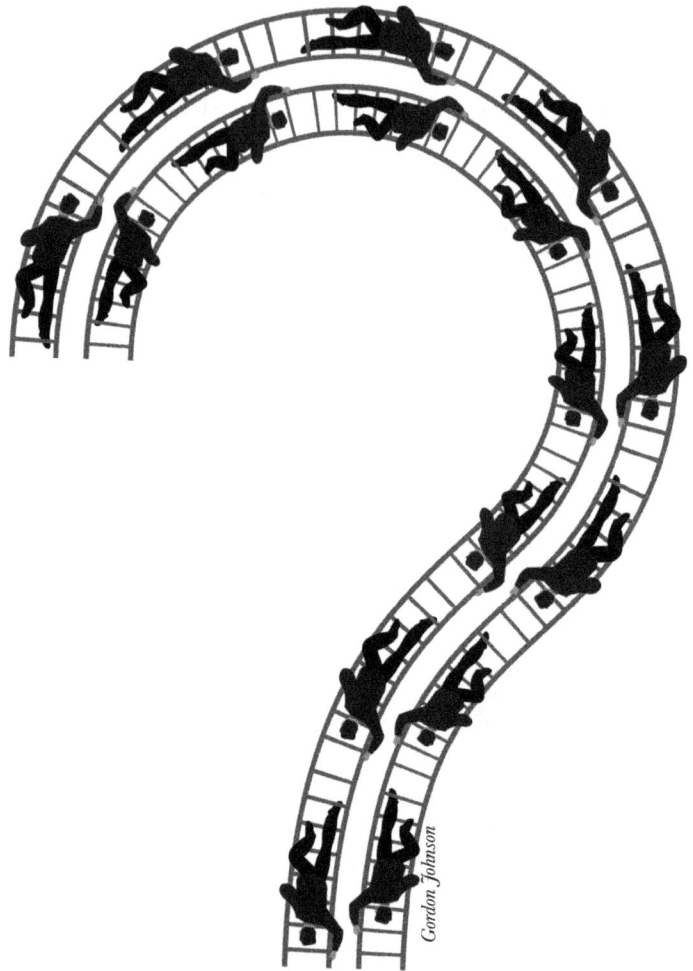

Gordon Johnson

Rosy / Bad Homburg / Germany

91

Sharing an opinion

Expressing your opinion allows your followers to understand your values and beliefs.

92

Share a reflective post

Share a meaningful post to communicate
the reasoning behind your actions with
your followers.

Megan Rexazin Conde

93

Respond to a question from Quora on social media

Responding to questions from Quora on social media allows for cross-platform engagement and demonstrates your expertise to a wider audience.

200 Degrees

94 Engage with tags or mentions

Engage with those who have tagged or mentioned you by responding to them in a post.

95

Share a snippet from a blog post

Share a captivating summary of a blog post rather than
just a link to entice your audience.

inke32

96 Sharing a chart, like a customer satisfaction chart for the product.

This provides visual evidence of the product's performance and customer feedback, which can enhance credibility and trust among your audience. By showcasing positive feedback and addressing any areas for improvement, you demonstrate transparency and a commitment to customer satisfaction. This not only engages your audience but also encourages interaction and discussion, ultimately strengthening your brand's presence on social media platforms.

97 Share a conversation

Send a picture of a social media conversation (with permission) and add your own thoughts to the conversation.

Courtesy of Cottonbro Studio

98 Event

Promote a relevant industry event, which may be conducted live online.

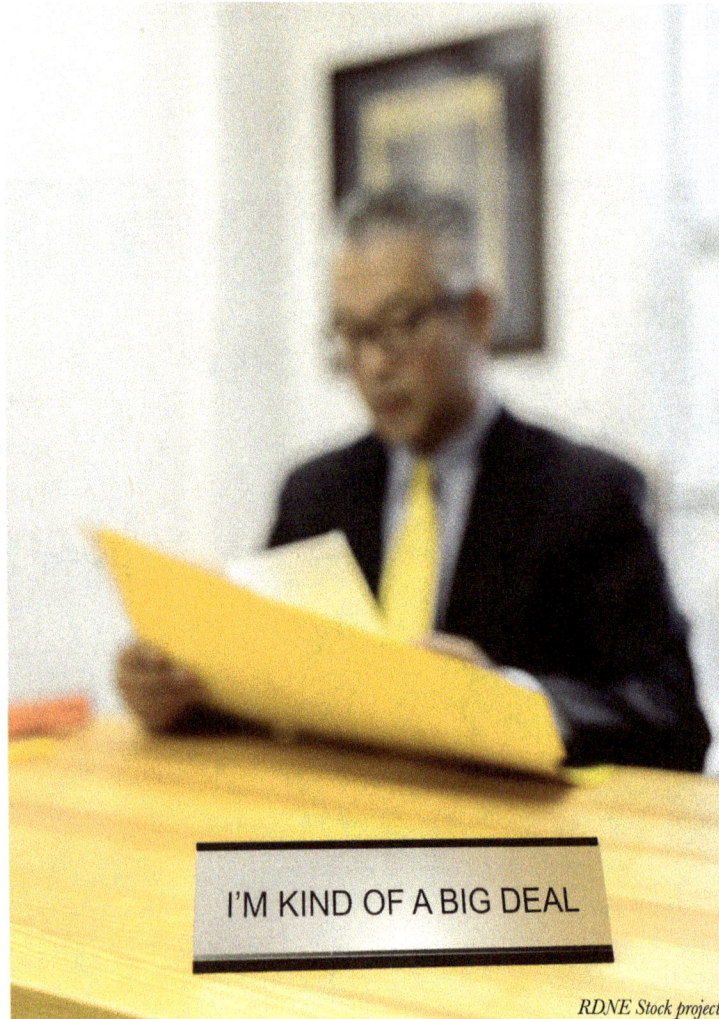

I'M KIND OF A BIG DEAL

RDNE Stock project

Amina Filkins

99

Share an amusing business anecdote.

Share a humorous anecdote from your business experiences. Post something that will evoke nostalgia and laughter among your fans or followers.

100 Data-Driven Report

Preparation of a report detailing methods and procedures for enhancing products and services is essential. This demonstrates your dedication to improving the quality of the product or service.

Courtesy of Walls.io

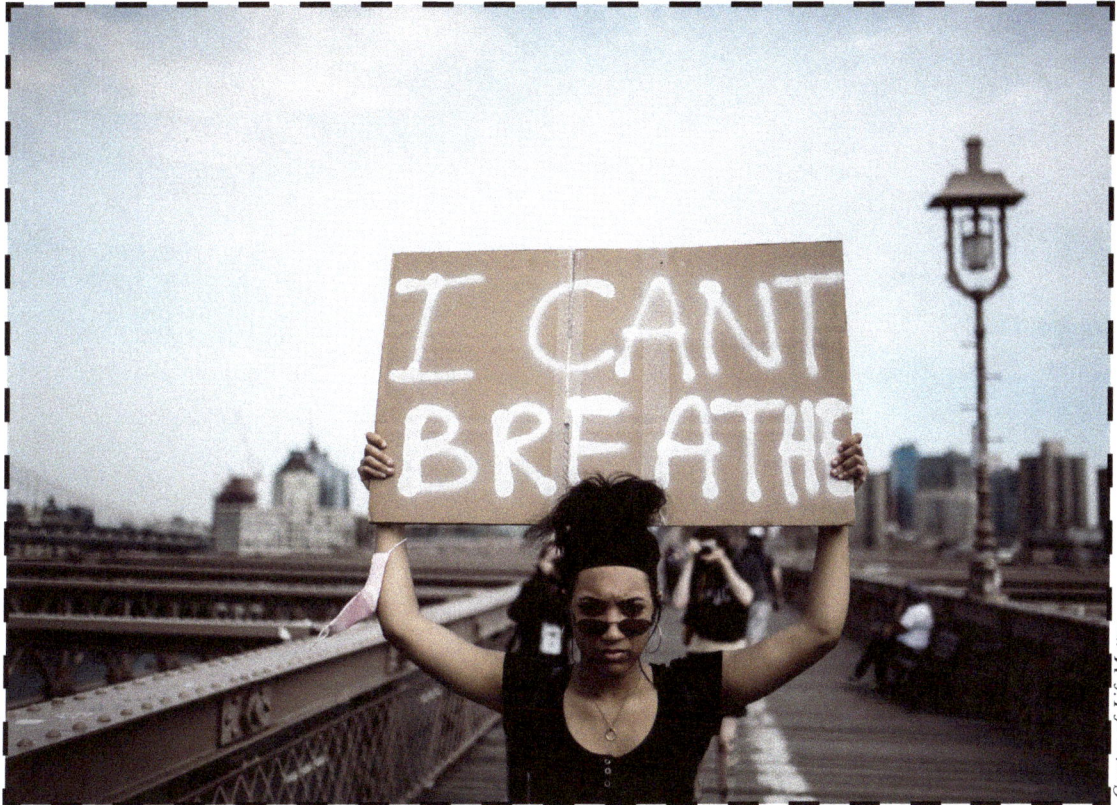

Courtesy of Life Matters

101 Share meaningful photos capturing your engagement in social responsibility initiatives.

Share impactful images showcasing your engagement in social responsibility endeavors. This tool wields significant influence, capable of both constructive and destructive outcomes, yet operates with utmost transparency and potency.

$$-\overset{F}{\underset{M}{\times}}-$$

www.ingramcontent.com/pod-product-compliance
Lightning Source LLC
Chambersburg PA
CBHW060926210326
41597CB00042B/4610